W9-BTO-321

3 4028 08503 8728
HARRIS COUNTY PUBLIC LIBRARY

J 629.225 Osi
Osier, Dan
Bulldozers

$8.25
ocn843785209
09/09/2014

First edition.

BULLDOZERS

Dan Osier

PowerKiDS press.

New York

Published in 2014 by The Rosen Publishing Group, Inc.
29 East 21st Street, New York, NY 10010

Copyright © 2014 by The Rosen Publishing Group, Inc.

All rights reserved. No part of this book may be reproduced in any form without permission in writing from the publisher, except by a reviewer.

First Edition

Editor: Amelie von Zumbusch
Book Design: Andrew Povolny

Photo Credits: Cover Jelle vd Wolf/Shutterstock.com; p. 5 Jan van Broekhoven/Shutterstock.com; p. 7 Guido Akster/Shutterstock.com; p. 9 Asaf Eliason/Shutterstock.com; pp. 11, 15, 17, 23 iStockphoto/Thinkstock; p. 13 Tomasz Pietryszek/Photodisc/Getty Images; p. 19 JoLin/Shutterstock.com; p. 21 Jupiterimages/Photos.com/Thinkstock.

Library of Congress Cataloging-in-Publication Data

Osier, Dan.
 Bulldozers / by Dan Osier. — First edition.
    pages cm. — (Construction site)
 Includes index.
 ISBN 978-1-4777-2859-8 (library binding) — ISBN 978-1-4777-2952-6 (paperback) —
 ISBN 978-1-4777-3029-4 (6-pack)
 1. Bulldozers—Juvenile literature. I. Title.
 TA725.O85 2014
 629.225—dc23
                    2013015809

Manufactured in the United States of America

CPSIA Compliance Information: W14PK3: For Further Information contact Rosen Publishing, New York, New York at 1-800-237-9932

Contents

Bulldozers are cool! They move dirt and other things.

Some are used in construction. Others are used in mines or on farms.

Some armies use them. The nickname for an Israeli Army one is a Doobi.

They are slow. The fastest ones go just 18 miles per hour (29 km/h).

Bulldozers tend to have **tracks**. These keep bulldozers from sinking into soft soil.

13

The **blade** is in front. It pushes things.

There are three kinds of blades. They are the S blade, the U blade, and the S-U blade.

Some bulldozers have **rippers**.
They are on the back. They tear
up dirt.

19

Many companies make bulldozers. Caterpillar makes the most.

21

Have you ever seen a bulldozer?

Harris County Public Library
Houston, Texas

WORDS TO KNOW

blade   ripper   track

WEBSITES

Due to the changing nature of Internet links, PowerKids Press has developed an online list of websites related to the subject of this book. This site is updated regularly. Please use this link to access the list: www.powerkidslinks.com/cs/dozers/

INDEX